Multiple Bird Households

Linda S. Rubin

Distributed in the UNITED STATES to the Pet Trade by T.F.H. Publications, Inc., 1 TFH Plaza, Neptune City, NJ 07753; on the Internet at www.tfh.com; in CANADA by Rolf C. Hagen Inc., 3225 Sartelon St., Montreal, Quebec H4R 1E8; Pet Trade by H & L Pet Supplies Inc., 27 Kingston Crescent, Kitchener, Ontario N2B 2T6; in ENGLAND by T.F.H. Publications, PO Box 74, Havant PO9 5TT; in AUSTRALIA AND THE SOUTH PACIFIC by T.F.H. (Australia), Pty. Ltd., Box 149, Brookvale 2100 N.S.W., Australia; in NEW ZEALAND by Brooklands Aquarium Ltd., 5 McGiven Drive, New Plymouth, RD1 New Zealand; in SOUTH AFRICA by Rolf C. Hagen S.A. (PTY.) LTD., P.O. Box 201199, Durban North 4016, South Africa; in Japan by T.F.H. Publications. Published by T.F.H. Publications, Inc.

Manufactured in the
United States of America
by T.F.H. Publications, Inc.

Contents

More Than One

Although keeping and caring for one pet bird is relatively easy, it can be an entirely different situation when an owner acquires one or more new birds. Many owners enjoy having a second bird in their care because it can provide company for their original pet when they're not around. Often times, however, two is not enough. It is not uncommon to hear of one-bird families growing into two-bird families, then three, then four, and so on.

When acquiring additional birds, especially of different species, there are many factors to consider—compatibility, housing requirements, varying nutritional needs, taming and training, health care, and, possibly, the joys of hobby breeding. Keeping companion birds, like keeping other pets, can affect an owner's life and bring a calming influence and profound happiness. The opposite may be true when an owner is not prepared for the time and commitment involved in a growing avian family. However, when each new bird is chosen wisely and introduced responsibly, most negative problems can be avoided so that avian life remains trouble-free. The following chapters are meant to help facilitate that process and give insight into the art of keeping birds.

Starting a Collection

I f this is the first time you are purchasing a bird, it is generally recommended that you start with a species that is relatively easy to feed, house, and maintain. There are many species from which to choose, each with their own attributes. Take time to consider your lifestyle, housing arrangements, and other factors that may influence your decision. The choices are abundant—from small singers to great squawkers, and everything in between.

Before buying a bird, or adding one to a collection, learn all you can about the species you intend to purchase. Be certain that you will be able to provide all the requirements necessary for your new bird, especially if you are adding a new species you have yet to gain experience with. Consider whether you can provide the proper diet and the correct type of caging and accessories, as well as whether the new bird will require separate accommodations, live with others in an aviary, or live in a flight with mixed species. Consider your new bird's needs, but also protect the welfare and safety of the birds in your existing collection. Finally, should you choose to keep birds of both genders in the same species, you may want to decide if you will venture into the avicultural pursuit of hobby breeding.

Finches and Canaries

Canaries are highly recommended for their unrivaled ability to sing; they are affordable, easily available, and bred in many varieties. Finches are touted for their easy upkeep, and some species are relatively easy to breed and comfortably house in mixed collections. Though both finches and canaries do not require a lot of room, they must still have adequate flight space in which to exercise and move around.

Canaries have long been favored for their affordability as well as their ability to sing.

Softbills

Some softbilled birds, such as Mynah birds, can be taught to build impressive vocabularies, while other softbilled birds rarely talk. All have very specialized needs in their diet, care, and housing that must be met in order for them to thrive. Many of the softbilled birds, finches, and similar species do better with livefood additions such as mealworms, bee pollen, and other insect proteins as a regular part of the diet. If you plan to keep outdoor birds in a planted aviary or garden, then softbilled birds may be for you.

Parrots

If you'd like to keep an interactive species that can be tamed, taught to talk, and can become part of the family, then a member of the parrot family is highly recommended. Parrots come in all shapes and sizes, from the smallest members—the popular budgerigar or parakeet (as it is known in the United States), the feisty parrotlet, and the well-known lovebird—to the largest members—the Amazons, cockatoos, and macaws—and the many in between. Should your selection be a parrot, it is generally best for beginners to start with either a budgerigar or a cockatiel, and to learn about keeping these smaller, less expensive members of the parrot family before deciding upon one of the larger parrots and their higher maintenance care.

Budgerigars

Budgerigars, or budgies, make excellent family pets; they are easily tamed while young, and they come in nearly every color of the rainbow. They are highly social birds; they do well with either people or in groups of other budgies and sometimes with other small parrots, provided they are given adequate space. They can make excellent talkers—sometimes boasting a vocabulary of 100 to 200 words if properly taught—although their voice is diminutive and not as clear as larger birds. As babies, the normal colored varieties have black lines across their foreheads, and are known as "barheads" until they are 10 to12 weeks old and begin to lose the

With their bright and colorful feathers, Gouldian finches make a vibrant addition to a growing finch collection.

forehead stripes. As with most baby parrots, the black tips on their beaks will eventually disappears after the baby molt. Because baby budgies wean and are fully independent of their parents between 38 to 42 days old, it is best to obtain your budgie as close to this age as possible in order to start the taming process. Trained budgies are wonderful family birds, staying animated and involved in family indoor activities. Budgies are also considered the easiest bird to breed in the entire parrot family, provided that their basic needs are met.

Expert Advice

Although budgies are very social, they are highly territorial and will need to be removed and housed separately if seen to bother other birds; they may even attack and kill other birds in the enclosure.

Although they are extremely talented mimics, Mynah birds, like other softbills, have special dietary needs that must first be considered.

The ever-popular budgerigar, or "parakeet" as it is known in the United States, is a great bird for beginners and for those who want more than one bird.

Budgies may be housed in a collection with other budgies, as long as they have enough room to escape from each other, as they can frequently argue in long squawking sessions. Both sexes can become aggressive when in breeding condition, and because budgies are nonseasonal breeders, this can occur at any time of the year. Some fanciers keep an aviary of small parrots or larger parakeets, and even some finches and doves, in a mixed collection with budgies. However, care must be taken not to allow budgies to monopolize the feed and water vessels, or harass other birds in the flight (even those that are sometimes larger than they are!).

Cockatiels

Though the budgerigar is the top-selling pet bird, found in more than 6 million American households, the cockatiel ranks a close second. With its wonderful personality, sweet

Cockatiels are gentle and devoted birds that make good pets for families with children.

Those looking for a small parrot-type bird should consider a lovebird; however, Peachface lovebirds should be given ample space if housed together.

disposition, numerous color mutations, and gentle nature, the cockatiel is a popular family favorite. It is easy to breed, makes a devoted companion bird, and, unlike the budgie, greatly enjoys having its neck and crest feathers gently stroked. A handfed cockatiel makes an ideal pet and will seek out its owner's company, readily perching on its owner's hand or shoulder. Such a bird is highly recommended as a first parrot-type bird and is especially safe with children.

Lovebirds

Another small parrot favorite is the lovebird. Unfortunately misnamed, the popular Peachface lovebird can become quite pugnacious toward other lovebirds if housed together in close quarters. Although a loving pet if handfed, a close eye must also be kept on the Peachface lovebird if it is housed with any other species. Other species of lovebirds are not quite as aggressive.

Medium-size Parrots

Other popular favorites include the medium-size birds, such as the many species of conures, mini-macaws, and the less available birds in the lory family. The larger parakeets, such as the *Psittacula* genus, with their long tapering tails, include the favorite Indian Ringnecks and Plumhead parakeets, and the *Neophema* genus—the Bourke, Turquoisine, and Scarlet-chested parakeets—all of which can be tamed while young but offer a little more challenge to breed than smaller birds.

The slightly larger, stockier parrots, with their short, square tails, include the pionus parrots, the popular caiques, and African parrots such as the *Poicephalus* genus (Senegals,

The Turquoisine parakeet is a small and colorful bird that can be tamed when young.

Though not as showy as some other parrots, African Greys are sensitive birds that excel at talking.

Eclectus parrots are noted for their vivid coloration and unusual feathering, which appears as hair or fur and requires regular spray baths.

Meyers, Cape, etc.). These birds are on the quiet side, with engaging personalities, and make a good choice for the next "step up" from owning a cockatiel. However, it is always recommended to research the specific habits and characteristics before acquiring any species. For example, most conures from the genus *Aratinga,* although very colorful and engaging, can have an extremely shrill screeching call that tends to eliminate them as a choice for apartment dwellers. However, their slightly less colorful cousins, the *Pyrrhura* conures, are much quieter.

Large Parrots

Larger parrots are more expensive, but can make wonderful companion birds, providing owners understand the personality and requirements of the species they wish to obtain. It is usually best to maintain some of the smaller parrots first, for an extended period of time, before working toward the larger parrots. By keeping smaller parrots, you will become familiar with the basic needs of hookbilled birds, including nutritional necessities, caging requirements, and taming and training methods.

One of the most popular species, the African Grey parrot, *Psittacus erithacus,* may not be the most colorful parrot, but its excellent talking skills more than make up for its lack of color. These birds command enormous vocabularies, depending upon the amount of effort demonstrated by an owner.

The Eclectus parrot is one of the few sexually dimorphic parrots—the hen is predominantly scarlet and the male is green. Eclectus can be very sensitive birds and are recommended for those who have some experience working with larger birds.

Amazon parrots are excellent companion birds and can be quite independent if given

Amazon parrots are sought after for their playfulness, talking ability, and attractive colors; the Lilac-crowned Amazon is not as readily available as others.

the company of toys, the companionship of another bird, or even a mirror. There are a number of species of Amazons available, although like other parrots they are becoming more rare over time because they are no longer imported but must be bred in captivity. Some species, such as the popular Double Yellow-headed Amazon, *Amazona ochrocephala,* and the Yellow-naped Amazon, *Amazona ochrocephala parvipes,* may become very bonded as "one person birds." Other common species, such as Orange-winged Amazons, *Amazona amazonica,* and Red-lored Amazons, *Amazona autumnalis,* generally get along with all members of the family. As in any group of individuals, there are always exceptions.

Cockatoos are an excellent choice for fanciers who wish to keep a bird that can be

Though considered by many to be the "ultimate" macaw, the Hyacinth is extremely expensive and requires substantial housing due to its large size.

Like other cockatoos, the Umbrella cockatoo is an affectionate parrot that will beg for attention and companionship.

tamed but also enjoys being cradled and cuddled. Many of the large, white cockatoos such as the Sulphur-crested, Moluccan, and Umbrella enjoy taming and training; however, they can render their owners nearly deaf by the volume of their screeching if they choose to squawk. The smaller white cockatoos, although some nearly as expensive as the large ones, make an excellent compromise by trading down on beak size, screaming volume, and the amount of destruction a massive beak can bring to a room, not to mention a bite to the hand. Some of the small white cockatoos include the less expensive Goffin and the pricier Bare-eyed, and deep pink Galah, or Rose-breasted.

Largest of all are the many species of macaws—the Scarlet, Blue and Gold, Hyacinth, Military, Green-wing; with their long tails and large bodies, these birds require the most in housing and maintenance.

Selecting a Bird

Now that you are ready to choose your new bird, you need to locate a source that will sell you a healthy companion bird. Many of the better retail pet stores keep their birds in a separate room or behind glass enclosures, feeding them a variety of foodstuffs and working with the birds to keep them tame. Several of the magazines devoted to birds carry a list of breeders, state by state, some of which are included on the magazines' web sites. More and more bird breeders are advertising the young birds and breeders they have for sale on the Internet. Also, most breeders are happy to provide you with a birth certificate or pedigree card from their aviary listing the year and number imprinted on the bird's closed, coded leg band, which is applied to the chick while still in the nest. The leg band code serves to permanently identify the bird and provides the bird's date of birth. Wherever you choose to make your purchase, do not hesitate to ask for viable references that you can check.

Compatibility

It is recommended that you purchase your first bird and wait until you have trained it before proceeding to add birds to your growing flock. It will be well worth the wait, because once you establish a bond, a process that requires daily handling, time, and patience, your bird will remain tame even around other birds, provided you keep interacting with it.

Do some research on the species you plan to house together and learn whether they are likely to get along. As a general rule, large birds should not be added to a small bird's aviary and vice-versa. Extra cages may mean more work, but they also provide more safety. Small birds cannot defend themselves

Consider age when choosing a bird—an older bird may already be trained, but a younger bird may be more likely to bond with its owner.

against larger species, no matter how friendly your larger pet may appear. Although it may be amusing to watch a cockatiel that has established a loving relationship with an Amazon parrot enter the Amazon's cage, a careful eye should be kept on the birds at all times. A small nip from a large bird can prove dangerous. An angry nip from a large parrot can prove disastrous. It only takes one unfortunate incident.

Choosing A Healthy Bird

When choosing your first companion bird, no matter which species you select, always obtain a bird that is in top physical condition, brimming with good health. A healthy bird will have a better chance of tolerating the stress of moving to a new home, adjusting to a new environment, and bonding to you, his new owner, without the complications that illness can bring. Sick birds do not make good pets. They are generally unresponsive to their surroundings, indifferent to training, and do not learn to talk. Although some people tend to feel sorry for the "runt of the litter," unless you are an experienced birdkeeper, chances are a sick bird may never recover from its illness. Beyond the numerous, costly trips to the veterinarian, owners of sick birds must often endure the heartache of losing a new pet, which can be especially hard on any children in the family.

Healthy birds exude a glow of peak condition, high energy, and alert interest in their environment. Their feathers should be clean and sleek, held closely to the body, and they should create a

tight appearance without evidence of fluffed out, damaged, or soiled feathers. Bird show judges often refer to immaculate feather condition as being in top condition, indicating a bird in radiant good health. There should be no sign of feather loss or a large number of missing feathers, which may be evidence of feather-picking, a difficult habit to break. Some birds will show a few tiny pinfeathers, or perhaps a missing flight or short tail feather, indicating the normal molting process (when a bird sheds old feathers, replacing them with new ones). Birds undergoing heavy molts should be

Only healthy birds should be added to a collection. Clean and sleek feathers are an indication of a bird's good health.

watched with care and given extra nutritional support at this time.

General signs of poor health include decreased appetite; a sluggish, listless, or depressed appearance, sometimes accompanied by tucking the head or beak into the wing; and fluffed up body feathers in an attempt to stay warm. This is not to be confused with healthy birds tucking their beaks in their backs for a midday nap, or preparing to roost for the night. Common accompanying respiratory symptoms include sneezing; wheezing; discharge from the eyes, beak, or nares (nostrils); and tail pumping or a gaping beak, indicating labored breathing.

Certain species make better pets for those with children. Size, of course, is a consideration, as is temperament and trainability.

Droppings should be monitored closely, especially with new birds. A pasty vent or change in droppings can accompany a number of conditions. Any deviation in the form and consistency of normal droppings should be heeded as a possible warning sign of ill health. Owners should become familiar with their bird's droppings to know what is considered normal for their bird, and what is not, so they may recognize any changes and take action.

Prior to purchase, carefully examine the bird's cage and environment to determine if conditions are clean and that other birds in the room appear healthy. Food and water vessels should remain clean and full, and any toys should be void of droppings, foreign matter, or regurgitated material. A number of perches should be evident and vary in size. To ensure a strong foothold and prevent potential foot problems, there should be several perches of the correct diameter for that species. Birds routinely wipe their beaks against perches, as we would use a napkin, so perches should be clean and splinter-free at all times.

Always examine the droppings at the bottom of the cage to determine if they are the correct size, color, and consistency, and if their number is appropriate to the number of birds kept in the enclosure. New birds can be monitored by observing the number, color, and consistency of their droppings in a 24-hour period. Droppings should not be overly loose, discolored, engulfed by a wet ring of water, or contain blood.

Healthy, normal droppings are round, semi-solid, and forest-green, black, or brown, with a white, round center. Exceptions include birds adjusting to a new diet, birds on a predominantly

Expert Advice

A bird's droppings may be affected by the diet it is fed. For example, unless birds are given fresh fruits and vegetables on a regular basis, their droppings can appear more watery. Pelleted, or extruded diets, can turn droppings brown, or other colors. And, because birds drink more water while on pellets, a pelleted diet can make droppings appear looser than when fed a seed-based diet.

Examine a bird's cage and surroundings when shopping for a pet; perches, food cups, and water dispensers should be clean and plentiful.

pelleted diet, or birds infrequently fed fresh foods, which may make droppings appear runny. Odorous droppings are not uncommon in breeding birds or birds getting ready to lay eggs. The odor comes from the bacteria inside the vent of the hen, who withholds her droppings until she leaves the nest each morning and afternoon to eat and bathe, releasing the droppings in a chosen spot in an attempt to keep the nest clean.

Before purchasing a bird, locate an experienced bird handler or someone knowledgeable who can feel the bird's keel, or breastbone, positioned vertically down the bird's chest. The keel bone should never protrude or feel sharp to the touch, and the bird should feel "meaty" on either side without appearing obese. New owners may be fooled by viewing what appears to be a large, "fat and sassy" baby, only to discover the bird is quite thin underneath its layers of feathers. The best arrangement is to take the bird directly to a certified avian veterinarian who specializes in birds for a full avian checkup, with the option to return the bird within a specified time frame if recommended. Wherever the purchase takes place, whether from a pet store or a breeder, the buyer should inquire about return policies and any health guarantees that are offered. It is best to get any such agreements in writing to avoid possible misunderstandings.

Expert Advice

Do not assume you can return a bird if it should become ill, or worse, if it should die. Each store or breeder varies in their return policies, and some provide no guarantee at all. Ask for a signed contract to avoid any misunderstandings. Today, many sources provide health certificates guaranteeing that birds have received specific tests and vaccines against such diseases as polyoma virus, psittacine beak and feather disease, and chlamydia. If such testing was not provided, ask if you may bring the bird to your avian veterinarian to examine, with the option to return it should it prove ill, and be clear on the time frame for the return.

Quarantine

All new birds added to a household or aviary must be quarantined for a minimum period of 30 days, ideally 60 days, with a 90-day quarantine considered even safer. Quarantine should be held at a facility that does not house other birds. One option is to try to board a new bird with a friend, relative, or a neighbor close enough where you can visit and attend to the bird's needs each day. If a bird must be taken home for quarantine, try and keep it on a separate air system if at all possible. At the very least, quarantine any new bird in a separate room away from existing birds and do not allow existing birds to visit or land on a quarantine bird's cage. After servicing your existing birds, see to the needs of your new bird under quarantine *last*. Then change out of your clothes and shower before you return to your existing birds again.

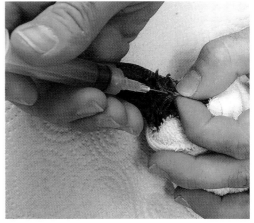

A visit to an avian veterinarian is a must before bringing any new bird home to your existing birds; be prepared for testing and a period of quarantine.

Quarantine is the only way to safeguard existing birds, from contracting illness from a new arrival. It also allows you to observe a new bird, convert it to your chosen avian diet, and acclimate the new bird before it is placed with existing birds, where it may have to battle for social position in the pecking order. If the bird is to be a tame companion, the time spent in quarantine allows you a period to get to know each other and become acquainted before serious training begins.

Because birds are experts at hiding illness, lest they fall prey to predators in the wild, by the time a bird shows signs of illness it may already be quite ill. Therefore, new birds should be tested even if they appear healthy, to be certain they are not covering up illness. If a number of birds are to be added together to a collection, then several birds at random should be tested. Seek out an avian veterinarian who specializes in the treatment of birds, because not all veterinarians are knowledgeable about avian species. The Association of Avian Veterinarians (see Resources) can recommend an avian veterinarian closest to your town.

The initial visit to the veterinarian will include a physical exam, where a bird is wrapped in a towel for its own protection while the veterinarian listens to its heart and lungs, palpates its breastbone, feels the body for lumps, and examines the vent, feathers, and wings. The veterinarian should also examine the oral cavity (mouth) with a pen light, as well as the eyes, nares (nostrils), and beak. After the exam, the bird is weighed and its weight and other results are recorded in its personal file. This baseline can be very important to future visits should they be necessary.

Routine tests performed during an initial exam can include a gram stain, cloacal culture, chemistry profile, and possibly testing for chlamydia, candida, and others, if warranted.

The costs of a bird's initial examination and follow-up testing should be considered as part of the purchase price of a bird; the initial time and expense of testing new arrivals is far less costly than the higher cost of treating an entire flock of infected birds.

Housing the Flock

Once you select your new bird, you must decide upon appropriate caging. Size, shape, and other specifications vary greatly from species to species, so before making any initial investment in equipment, do some preliminary research to learn about any individual requirements your new pet (or pets) may have.

Cages and Aviaries

As a general rule, a bird should be able to move completely around in its cage and fully stretch its wings. Birds fly back and forth, not up and down, so the longer the cage, the better. Regardless of size, any cage can become a prison, so regularly scheduled time outside the cage is critical. Daily exercise will keep a bird healthy, psychologically and physically, improving muscle tone and empowering the immune system.

Today, many materials are available—from brass and chrome cages to wrought iron parrot enclosures. It is best to select a cage that you can easily clean and disinfect. If painted, be certain that the paint is lead-free, as lead is extremely toxic to birds. If the cage is made of welded wire, the wire must be thoroughly washed to remove any zinc residue, which is another dangerously toxic substance to birds.

Be certain that the wire spacing is of the appropriate size for the species you select. For example, cockatiels can catch their heads in most cages with bars spaced for parrots and can end up hanging themselves, so it is imperative to ask for cockatiel barring in the cage that is selected.

Birds that are ground feeders in the wild, such as cockatiels and many of the larger, long-tailed parakeets, can also get their heads caught in the bottom grids when attempting to reach through for a fallen tidbit. It may therefore be best to remove the cage grid at the bottom of the cage to prevent this.

If space is a factor in your home, consider whether you have room for more than one cage or, perhaps, a very large cage.

Small finches, such as the Strawberry finch, are so tiny that they can escape through some of the smallest wire cages, so special care must be taken to choose an appropriate cage. On the other hand, parrots, with their massive beaks, can often chew their way out of some cages, so tougher materials should be used.

Cages should be placed in a draft-free location. Birds are extremely susceptible to drafts and can quickly develop respiratory ailments, so this is of paramount importance. Drafts come in many forms, from open windows, fans, and air conditioners, to heating vents and open doorways. If in doubt, move the cage. Covering half the cage can also be useful with a bird that prefers some protection from air currents along with some area for privacy.

Elimination of drafts is critical, but attention to air temperature is also important. Birds, like people, generally do best in an average room temperature of 68° Fahrenheit. Birds do not need hothouse temperatures. What is important is the constancy of the temperature. It is unhealthy to have any sudden rise or fall of temperature, which can lead to overheating or chills. An extreme decrease or increase in temperature can adversely affect birds, so any deliberate change in temperature must be carried out gradually.

In addition to selecting a draft-free location, the cage should be kept off the ground at eye level or higher, and out of reach of other animals or small children. A new bird may do better in a quiet bedroom where it can calmly settle in for a few days or adjust through a quarantine period.

Stock the cage with all its feed cups and necessary utensils prior to placing the bird inside. If using fountain style feeders, check the fountains every day to be certain that the flow of seed is not blocked. Keep toys at a minimum until a bird becomes used to its new surroundings and to you. Hanging millet spray nearby will usually entice a new bird to begin eating.

When adding different size birds to a cage or aviary, be certain you have enough perches for every bird to roost comfortably without feeling cramped or having to squabble to defend its territory. Perches should be of the correct size for all the birds in the aviary. To determine proper perch size, examine each bird's foot and check the grip it has around the perch. If the bird's foot grasps the perch firmly, showing all toes encircling the perch without toenails meeting or touching others, then it is generally the right diameter. Perches of different diameters within the cage will also help to exercise the feet and prevent foot problems from developing in the future.

It is easier on birds' feet to use natural tree branches, which birds also enjoy as a source of minerals when they strip the bark from the branches. Use only safe branches such as eucalyptus, willow, apple, maple, beech, oak, and other harder woods for the largest parrots—the cockatoos and macaws—whose massive beaks can destroy other branches with ease. Avoid cherry branches and others that are known to be toxic. Be certain to wash all branches thoroughly before attaching them inside an aviary in order to remove possible pesticides and other foreign material.

There should be enough food and water available to birds housed together, to avoid any fighting or monopolizing by more dominant individuals. Use only vessels that are appropriate for your birds; that is, specifically designed for that species. Place food and water vessels away from any areas where they may become soiled or fouled by droppings, such as under perches or toys. To prevent birds from being exposed to bacteria, a forerunner of disease, water cups should be checked often, cleaned, and refilled whenever necessary.

Size, bar spacing, accessories, and location must all be thought about when choosing a cage for a pet bird.

As a general rule, cleaning should be done as often as necessary. Some single cages may require cleaning on a daily basis; larger flight cages may go for a longer period. Use clean, completely dry newspaper (avoid color ink, which can be toxic), plain brown paper bags, cedar or pine chips, or packaged, dried corncob bedding. Should you select corncob, be certain to change it immediately if it becomes wet, or mold could begin to grow. Newspaper that is set aside for a minimum of three days while its ink completely dries is a common choice of bedding for cage bottoms and even larger aviaries. Newspaper is inexpensive, can be stored for long periods of time, and can be changed often and frequently.

Never overcrowd a cage or aviary by keeping too many birds together. Overcrowding can lead to stressful confrontations, aggressive behavior, and disease by weakening the immune system. There should be enough space for birds to fly and comfortably move around. Birds kept in single cages should have an opportunity to come out of the cage and exercise on a daily basis. Daily exercise will lengthen the longevity of a bird's life and keep it healthy and better able to fight off disease.

Toys and Accessories

Birds are fortunate today, thanks to the number of toys on the market produced by a growing number of creative manufacturers. With hundreds of styles to choose from, there is certainly a toy for every type of bird out there. By experimenting with different toys, you will soon learn which kind your bird prefers. There is no doubt that each bird you own will certainly have a preference for one toy or another, whether

Expert Advice

Always examine the materials toys are made of. Be certain that colored wood is made from nontoxic food coloring, and that any chain links are completely closed. Be extra vigilant when considering the purchase of "homemade toys" not produced by a larger manufacturer.

In a cage with multiple birds, there should be enough food and water cups for all; watch to see that all birds have equal access.

colored blocks of wood, chewable rawhide, chains and bells, plastic shapes, or any of the numerous combinations now available.

Toy safety is one of the most important lessons to learn early on. Though most toy manufacturers are usually careful to only produce safe toys, owners must also use common sense. For example, be sure to offer toys that are the correct size for the bird you own. You would never give a cockatiel toy to a macaw or large cockatoo, whose massive beak could rip it apart, and who could choke on the broken parts. Big birds should only be given toys made specifically for their size. This may cost more initially, but it is well worth the precaution, because the resulting veterinary bills would certainly be even more expensive.

Toys offer a wonderful way for your birds to play and entertain themselves while you are away. Be sure to change your birds' toys periodically, rotating them every so often unless there is a particular favorite that a bird is attached to. By rotating toys you prevent boredom. Try not to overcrowd the cage with so many toys that your bird cannot move around and stretch.

The addition of toys can be a successful deterrent to feather-plucking and will help distract a bird from neurotically picking at its own feathers when alone. Toys are also good company if you are unable to provide a companion bird, or if you are not available. Toy mirrors, especially, can provide additional companionship because birds do not understand they are seeing their own reflection and believe they are looking at another bird. However, toys should never be thought of as a total substitute for your company. If you can no longer give your parrot the attention it deserves, it may be kinder to find someone who can or to buy a companion for your bird.

Schedules and Lighting

Birds are creatures of habit. They feel most comfortable when they are fed and watered at the same time each day and when their cages are cleaned on a regular basis. Birds learn to trust their handlers by relying on this routine, which over time builds confidence. As the owner and caregiver of your birds, you are completely responsible for your birds' health and well-being. Your birds totally rely upon you for healthy food, fresh water, and clean surroundings. It is your responsibility to make certain that your birds' requirements are being met.

In addition to food and water, your birds need to receive enough sleep each night in order to maintain good health. Keeping birds up past bedtime can wear them down, stress their immune system, and, over time, lead to illness. In the wild, birds wake and sleep with the cycle of the sun. In captivity, we provide artificial lighting to extend this cycle. Breeders who wish their birds to breed indoors take advantage of artificial lighting to create the breeding season. However, birds should routinely be awake during daylight hours, and at night receive nearly as many hours of sleep as it is dark outside. This may mean 10 to 12 hours of sleep, or more, in order for some birds to feel at their peak.

The easiest method of guaranteeing a good night's sleep is to put your birds' lamp on a timer. Set the timer so that the lamp will go on around dusk and turn off after a few hours to ensure a final feed and the opportunity to find perch space for the night. Some timers come with dimmers so that the onset and shutdown of the lamp will be gradual and will gently ease the birds into light or darkness. If your birds are kept outside, they will rise and sleep with the natural setting of the sun.

Take advantage of all of the space in a cage by putting perches and toys at all levels; birds often prefer the top of a cage to the bottom.

The quality of daylight hours is just as important as sleep. Some bird owners who keep their collection of birds in one room invest in full spectrum florescent lighting, which duplicates sunlight. Birds that are kept outdoors also gain the natural advantage of receiving vitamin D_3 when exposed to the sun. Care must also be taken so that birds are not allowed to overheat. Frequent baths provided by sprinkler systems, pressure pumps, or clean atomizers, used only for spraying birds and for no other purpose, often provide relief when it gets unbearably hot. Hanging wet sheets near aviaries is also effective.

Night Fright

Whether your birds are kept inside or outdoors, it is important to provide a source of artificial light at night to prevent night fright from occurring. Night fright can have disastrous effects on birds, as it may send them into a frenzy, causing them to panic and crash into walls or cage bars. This can occur when unforeseen events happen, such as light shining in a window from car head-lights, the noise of a car backfiring, even a dog, cat, or wild animal peering into a window. It is usually best to draw curtains at night to prevent such things from happening. However, some owners have conditioned their birds to sleep and to rise with the sun, not using curtains; this may be more successful if the environment outside the window is not a busy one.

Because birds tend to panic during night frights, it is best to prevent it altogether by using a night light, or lamp with low wattage, left on at night so that birds may orient themselves in the dark.

Expert Advice

Birds that are kept outside in a flight can also hurt themselves by flying into cage wire. Try putting up netting several feet from each end of the aviary so that fast flyers are stopped by it before they crash into the wire. This works well for aviaries that are exceptionally long.

The size and strength of your birds will determine which toys are best for them. A cockatoo, for example, can easily destroy a toy designed for a budgie.

Some owners of indoor birds keep a lamp with a 15-watt bulb in an adjacent room during the night; or a night light within the room where the birds are housed. Experiment with wattage until you find one that will not keep birds up all night, but will shed enough light to allow them to navigate in their cage. Should night fright occur, it is best to turn on the lights to allow the birds to see where they are flying. It generally takes several minutes for birds to calm down and settle back on to their perches. After they have settled in and resumed roosting, you can turn the light back down.

Introducing a New Bird

After you have completed a quarantine period for your new arrival and have moved the bird into the same room with your existing bird or birds, place the new bird's cage nearby. Never put a new bird into another bird's cage without a period of introduction so the birds can get to know each other. Most birds are social creatures, eating, drinking, breeding, and traveling together in flocks; however, they are familiar with each member of the flock and usually have a hierarchy of dominance that maintains order within the flock. The same theory applies to any new birds you introduce. Usually, the more established bird, or birds, will have higher rank or dominance within the flock and will assert this dominance upon any newcomers.

The best way to make an introduction is to place a cage nearby or next to another bird, taking care not to allow them to touch should you observe any aggression. For example, should one bird lunge forward with its beak while the other is defensively waving its foot, this may provide the opportunity for its toenail, toe(s), or foot to be caught in the beak of the aggressive bird. Birdkeepers are familiar with a well-known philosophy from Murphy's Law: "If you think it won't happen, it usually will." Therefore, always be prepared for the worst, and hopefully these precautions will pay off in a safe environment for your birds.

During this period of time you should keep your new bird inside its cage while working with your existing birds. Once tame, you can take your new bird out for its regular playtime. If you have birds that are of the same species, or of similar size and demeanor, you may consider the possibility of having them share the same cage. There are many valid reasons for housing birds together. Keeping birds in the same cage can provide companionship for birds during those times when you are away; birds can groom or preen one another and play together; keeping birds together can prevent neurotic behaviors such as feather-plucking, screaming, or self-mutilation. Birds are highly social, so many species, especially the larger parrots, can form strong bonds and may wish to breed should conditions be right.

Once your new bird has bonded with you, you might try letting it outside the cage with your existing bird, providing the new bird will not be harmed by much larger or aggressive species. For example, as a rule it would be unwise to allow your new Amazon parrot out with a more defenseless cockatiel; however, there can be exceptions. Some of the oddest "couples" or partnerships can be formed in the avian world, usually due to a social need to bond to another bird, although its usually between birds of similar size. In any case, it is imperative that you supervise such birds when they are at liberty outside the cage, to be certain that neither could endanger the other.

Play gyms or stands, which can usually be moved around, are an excellent way to provide your bird with exercise and time out of its cage.

Should your goal be to house the birds together in one cage, you have two methods from which to choose. If the birds get along from the start, for example, courtship feed, preen one another, or visit each other's cage without evidence of warfare, then it is relatively easy. Simply allow the birds to select the cage they prefer and remove the second cage. This method might be preferred by some smaller birds such as cockatiels, which grow especially attached to their cages and can become extremely upset over any changes and even lose their appetite for several days. Therefore, continued monitoring of the situation is recommended.

If selecting one of the existing cages for both birds, make certain that one of the birds is not monopolizing the feed or water dishes or harassing the other bird in any manner. This is especially important the first few days. Never lock birds in together and go away for a weekend, or go off to work for extended hours, without first having tested whether the birds will get along.

Observing the birds closely and monitoring the number of droppings at the bottom of the cage should reveal whether both birds have eaten their fill. Also, check their crops at bedtime. If your birds are tame, you can pick them up just before bedtime and check that their crop area is bulging (the area under their throat and above their breast); the crop will also look well rounded from a profile view.

The second and more popular method is to introduce the birds to neutral territory. This is easier and safer, although a bit more expensive because it involves the added cost of a new cage. Simply purchase a new cage, large enough to comfortably house the birds, then put the birds in together at the same time. This gives each bird a fair chance to establish itself and discover the new territory. The first method gives an unfair advantage to the bird that previously lived in the residence and might treat the newcomer as an unwelcome intruder. With the second method, both birds are on equal footing, without one having any advantage over the other. Still, it bears warning to closely watch the birds to be certain that they are getting along and that harmony prevails.

When introducing a pair of birds, watch carefully for signs of aggression.

Whichever method you choose, it is always best to make any changes when you will be able to stay in the aviary or room for an extended period of time, such as a long weekend. Many a tragedy can be prevented with observation, care, and forethought.

Flock Control

The methods previously covered can also apply when housing flocks together. Birds may be introduced into an existing flight already housing one or more birds; or all birds, current and new, may be transferred to a new flight cage or aviary at the same time. It is usually a matter of individual circumstances that determine which method is chosen.

Sometimes, aggressors within a community may be identified. Due to hormonal changes, or atmospheric pressure and seasonal changes, some birds may be thrown into a breeding cycle, whether intended or not. Some species are known for their aggression or dominance of one gender over another gender. For example, species in the genus *Psittacula,* such as Indian Ringneck parakeets, Plumheads, and others, traditionally have female dominance over males, and the female is receptive to the male only during the breeding season. Many times, single birds in a flight will not harm other birds, but they can attack and kill less aggressive birds in the same flight when paired (e.g., Plumheaded parakeets or Peachface lovebirds).

Birds that are raised together from a young age are more likely to get along than those that are brought together at an older age.

A group of new birds should not be left alone until they have shown that they are compatible.

Such consideration should be made when housing more gentle species like cockatiels, some common finches, and doves, which are unable to protect themselves against such aggressors that are acting on instinct to eliminate any other "rival" from their "territory."

Although clipping the wings of aggressors tends to slow them down, it may be safer to find them different housing if it is a mixed collection involving more docile birds. Breeders working with species from the *Psittacula* genus commonly clip the hen's wings so she will not kill her mate. However, it is usually the opposite concern in most other parrots. For example, the white cockatoos are known for killing their mates if they do not have the space to fly away, with the males oftentimes the aggressor. Wing clipping an aggressive bird may be an act that can often save the life of a cage mate.

Clipping the wings of an aggressive bird may help to control its behavior; those birds accustomed to being handled will be easier to clip.

Finally, some owners who are intent on breeding some of their birds may wish to utilize the flocking method. Commonly utilized by experienced breeders of large parrots, flocking your birds is a method where birds are all housed together in a very large aviary or flight and allowed to select and bond with a mate of their choosing, rather than a mate chosen by their owner. The pairs are then removed and separated for breeding in individual pens. Flocking often brings positive results when previous pairings fail to produce a bond between two birds.

Caring for the Flock

Nutrition is a much-debated topic among birdkeepers, with many differing opinions and practices. It is up to each owner to decide what and how they will feed their birds, keeping in mind that the birds' health is the most important element of the equation. Optimum nutrition directly affects a bird's health and longevity; nutritional deficiencies are frequently seen by avian veterinarians as the forerunner to disease.

Pellets

A host of manufacturers have developed avian pellets, granules, and extruded products that closely approximate the nutritional needs of cage birds as far as we know at this time. By now, it is commonly understood that seeds are deficient in most vitamins—with the exception of some of the B complex group—so pellets are a good choice because they provide well-rounded nutrition in each granule. Pellets come in all shapes and sizes, to appeal to different species of birds, and manufacturers go to great lengths to test their products on birds to ensure palatability.

Choices for small birds range from tiny pellets to crumbles. Pellets for the larger species can come in just about every color, shape, and size imaginable. If your local pet store does not carry pellets, ask them to contact a manufacturer and order them for you. Some distributors also make small samples available to their customers so they can test which pellets—and their size, shapes, and taste—appeal to their birds.

Once you obtain pellets for your birds it is critical that you follow the manufacturer's instructions to the letter for converting birds onto pellets, if your bird is not familiar with them. Mix pellets in with the bird's current food, which is gradually eliminated until the bird has fully converted over to the new food; sometimes conversions can take one to two weeks.

Pellets, seeds, nuts, and dried fruits and vegetables can all be combined for a healthy diet.

Seeds and Seed Blends

Some bird owners prefer to use a seed blend that they special order, find in a store, or create on their own. This is also an option for those that are unable to locate a pelleted diet. Always select a seed mix appropriate to the species you are feeding. Keep in mind that birds in mixed collections may have access to seeds meant for other species. For example, if keeping budgies together with larger birds, the budgies may steal the more fattening seeds such as hemp, niger, oats, and safflower, or have access to larger amounts of the same seeds than they were meant to have.

Delicious Millet

Whether feeding pellets or a seed mix, all birds relish panicum, best known as spray millet. These small golden millets are seed heads grown on sprays that are harvested intact on their stalks. They are prized by any species, both young or old, breeders and nonbreeders, and are especially attractive to sick birds that may eat nothing else, or to baby birds in the process of weaning; these birds may try the sprays first before more challenging and harder seeds. When feeding spray millet to mixed collections, provide enough sprays so all birds have a chance to sample them. It is always a pleasure to watch the birds feast upon the sprays and hear the aviary become silent as serious munching takes place. Larger birds such as the bigger cockatoos and macaws might appreciate another variety called megamillet, which carries larger red millet seeds. However, it may be a matter of individual preference to determine which spray variety a bird prefers, as even the larger birds have been known to prefer the smaller millet sprays.

Supplementation and Seeds

Be certain to find out what is in a seed mix and whether vitamins have been added. If the seed mix lacks vitamins, you will need to add a good multiple-vitamin/mineral supplement to your birds' diet. The best method of providing vitamins for your birds is to administer them in their ration of soft foods. Tests have demonstrated that adding vitamins to water has only limited success; the vitamins lose potency within a few hours, and bacteria may start to grow because the water is no longer clear. Also, some birds may drink very little water, so it is difficult to know just how much of the vitamins are being ingested. Instead, add the vitamin to your bird's daily ration of vegetables, foods, or other soft foods so it will be consumed immediately

Expert Advice

Birds must not go a day without eating, so always make certain that yours have a full crop before going to bed each night. If denied food for only a few days, they will not survive.

while the bird eats its special treat. Your avian veterinarian can advise you on which vitamin product to use. However, be certain that the brand you select contains vitamin D_3, which birds require. Vitamin D_3 is vital to the absorption and high blood levels of calcium and phosphorous; in addition to other functions, it helps to keep birds' skeletons strong and their beak and nails from becoming weak and rubbery.

Providing Produce

Fruits and vegetables are an important part of the diet of every bird. Fresh vegetables should be distributed to all, from finches to macaws, at least several times a week. Dark green, leafy vegetables, which are extremely high in vitamin A, or carotene (converted into vitamin A in the liver), include dandelion greens (and the flower), carrot greens, collards, kale, comfrey, and spinach. Greens that have moderate amounts of vitamin A but

Spray millet is a treat enjoyed by most birds—some like to hold it themselves, while others prefer to nibble from a piece clipped to the cage.

many other good nutrients include broccoli, mustard greens, Swiss chard, beet tops, chicory, escarole, parsley, and watercress. Other vegetables high in vitamin A include yams, carrots, red peppers, pumpkin, squash, and sweet potato. *Never* feed avocado—it is toxic to birds and can lead to death. Corn on the cob (or frozen thawed or canned corn niblets) is a special favorite and an excellent source of fiber.

Fruits are another favorite item and are especially relished by parrots, although other birds can be trained to eat small pieces of fruit, if fed frequently enough to become familiar with it. Popular fruits include apples, oranges, tangerines, pomegranates, papayas, mangos, berries (cranberries, blueberries, strawberries, blackberries, raspberries), cherries, melons (cantaloupe, honeydew, etc.), nectarines, peaches, pears, plums, lemons, limes, etc. Always remove large pits such as peach pits. Many times birds will eat small seeds, such as those found in apples, papayas, and pomegranates, without ill effect.

Fruits and vegetables can be fed several times a week, or daily to parrots. Produce provides excellent nutrition and helps amuse and entertain birds while they consume it. In order to train birds to eat their fruits and vegetables, they often need to be exposed to them while young. However, older birds can be trained to eat them,

Expert Advice

Research the special needs of the birds you keep together. Budgies, for example, need a source of iodine in their diet that other parrots do not need. Iodine, in Lugols solution, is available through your veterinarian.

Birds have greatly varying nutritional needs. This premium seed mix forms the basis of a healthy Gouldian finch diet, but would be virtually useless for a large parrot.

too, by repeatedly providing fresh food on a daily basis. It may take months; owners must be prepared to waste the amounts provided until one day the bird starts to sample them. But it is worth the effort, because fresh produce provides endless joy and nourishment for all birds. And, if your birds require a vitamin supplement, it can be added to their produce.

Table Foods

Table foods can also be included in a bird's diet, provided they do not include sugar, caffeine, chocolate, alcohol, or tobacco, as these can be deadly. Choose from the carbohydrate group (pastas, rice, noodles, macaroni, etc., all without the sauce); proteins such as cooked and deboned chicken, meat, fish, scrambled or hard-boiled eggs; and cooked vegetables that are not overcooked, which destroys vitamin content. Other favorites include whole wheat bread, spread sparingly with peanut butter (which can be fattening), or other healthy foods.

Cooked beans and legumes are an excellent source of protein; these include kidney beans, black beans, lima beans, pinto beans, split peas, chickpeas, and others. Beans can be slow cooked in advance, stored in the freezer, and thawed when needed. Bird breeders rely on a mix of cooked whole grain rice, corn, and beans, to which a vitamin supplement is added, which is given to breeding birds as a soft food to feed their young. Provide only as much as will be eaten in several hours and refill the mix as needed. Other leftover produce and table foods should be removed before bedtime.

Water

Water is an important element of an avian diet. It should be clean and fresh, and served cold on a daily basis. If droppings, food, or other materials foul the water, change it more frequently. Providing clean, uncontaminated drinking water helps prevent bacteria from forming.

Calcium

Calcium in adequate amounts is a critical addition to an avian diet. Seeds are deficient in their calcium content, so calcium must be provided in another form. Cuttlebone or mineral block should be made available at all times. Always be certain the soft side is facing inside the cage, and that the birds are actually eating the bone or block. Scraping a few ridges across the surface can create interest in the cuttlebone. African Grey parrots, especially, have a higher dietary need for calcium, so it is critical that they see a veterinarian to be certain that blood levels for calcium are acceptable.

Expert Advice

Imagine if you had to drink from the same water container as your birds—keep a clean supply of water available at all times.

Fresh fruits and vegetables should be provided to all birds, whether in the form of chopped greens for a Zebra finch, or as broccoli florets for a Blue-front Amazon.

Hobby Breeding

Sometimes bird owners with no intention of breeding their birds find that their birds have decided otherwise. Anxious hens may begin to scout out possible nesting sites, and formerly gentle males may become nippy, inflict bites, and become downright territorial. Springtime and other environmental conditions can bring on raging hormones, driving birds to reproduce as they were meant to if they were living in the wild.

It is not uncommon for hens that are single pets or who are unmated to start laying eggs. Some species, such as cockatiels, can become chronic egg-layers, which can lead to a life-threatening situation if continuous egg-laying depletes calcium reserves and causes egg-binding, prolapsed vents, or even ruptures into egg peritonitis. These situations require emergency care with an avian veterinarian who is familiar with treating such problems. However, if birds are well nourished, have developed egg-laying muscles through adequate opportunity to exercise, and are in good health, egg-laying should not bring about such emergencies.

Bird owners should decide whether they wish to allow birds the opportunity to breed, or wish to discourage it. Birds are stimulated to

Five-day-old White-face cockatiels. Babies that are taken from their parents require around-the-clock feeding and attention.

breed through environmental stimuli, which excite their hormone levels and encourage them to reproduce. In the wild such stimuli include an increased photolight period or additional daylight hours; increased rain, temperature, and humidity; an abundance of appropriate food such as seed heads in the "milky stage"; the presence of a suitable nesting site; and the acceptance of an appropriate mate.

In captivity, we sometimes provide these conditions and unwittingly subject birds to such overstimulation. Breeding behaviors can result from a combination of any of the following conditions: keeping birds up too late, exposing them to increased photolight periods; bathing and misting birds too often to imitate the humid conditions of increased rainfall; providing milky-stage foods such as soft foods on a daily basis; allowing birds to investigate possible nesting sites (these are always places you would never have guessed); and giving birds access to potential mates.

This is not to say that birds should not be bathed, well fed, or allowed exercise and visits with members of the opposite sex. Bird owners, however, can influence the environment to deter some of these factors that encourage

Breeding birds should be provided with special foods to help maintain good health during this very demanding time.

breeding. Merely reverse some of the conditions that stimulate breeding conditions. For example, cut back on the amount of daylight hours or artificial light by allowing your birds to go to bed earlier. Continue feeding fruits and vegetables, because produce supplies important vitamins and minerals, but cut back or eliminate the soft foods that resemble soaked seeds or seeds in their milky stage. Cut back on the amount of spray misting if you are bathing birds frequently and suspect that they find it too stimulating. Eliminate any obvious potential nesting sites and watch pairs during their time out together.

Should egg-laying occur, allow the hen to incubate the eggs at least one full week beyond the normal period. She will abandon them when she is ready to. If the hen has not been fertilized the eggs will not hatch. Pulling the eggs will only encourage the hen to replace them with a new clutch and further deplete her calcium reserves. In the wild, if a pair loses its eggs to predators, they are programmed to replace the loss with another round of eggs, biologically enabling their genes to survive through their future offspring.

If eggs are fertile and you wish to raise young, try not to move the eggs elsewhere because sometimes a young hen, especially an inexperienced one, will abandon them. Do not be tempted to open eggs prematurely. If you hear a chick peeping inside the egg, and should it be overdue and you wish to assist, gently open the egg around the circumference with a clean thumbnail or toothpick. If you see any sign of blood, or the membrane is not dry, return the egg immediately, as the chick is not ready to come out. It may require several more hours or days, depending upon when the hen first began to incubate the eggs full-time. Assisting a hatching is not normal and should only be done in an emergency. Strong, vital chicks usually have no trouble hatching on their own.

If your purpose is to begin hobby breeding, you should invest in a suitable nest box of the proper dimensions and attach it to the breed-

For convenience and ease, many cages are set up with feeding cups and accessories that can be filled and cleaned from outside the cage.

ing cage. Keep a careful watch to be certain the pair get along harmoniously. You will soon see the routine of the male taking up residence outside the nest entrance while the hen sits inside. In some species, the males relieve the hens during the early morning and late afternoon when the hen appears for a quick meal and a bath. Males will remain on guard outside the nest entrance at night.

Try to get the birds accustomed to your routine of inspecting the nest at the same time each day. However, when working with larger birds, or birds that become too nervous, it may be best to leave them alone or they may abandon or even injure eggs and young. If all is going well, you will know when the young have hatched by the unmistakable sound of peeping chicks and courtship feeding. If at all possible, try to obtain closed-coded leg bands from national avicultural societies (see Resources) to band your chicks so they will always carry your breeder's code and be able to be identified for life. Closed-coded bands are available through the avicultural societies at a small cost and can only be put on a chick when it is one to three weeks old, depending upon the species.

Hybridization

An important consideration whenever keeping birds together, especially closely related species of the opposite sex, is the possibility that they may breed. Hybridization should be discouraged, because it creates offspring that are not valued in aviculture. Hybrid offspring are not viable to existing gene pools, being of neither one species nor the other, so they are difficult to sell. They

Hybrid birds, such as this macaw, detract from existing gene pools and impede efforts to ensure a purebred species.

For some people, two birds are better than one. But the decision to add birds to your household should not be taken lightly.

cannot add to an aviculturist's breeding program, as hybrids will only impede a breeder's blood-lines; therefore, these birds are only suitable as pets.

Today, breeders are challenged with trying to reproduce the many species of parrots we have in aviculture before they are entirely lost to us. The reproduction of purebred species will only take place if hybrid breedings are avoided, because hybrids can only ensure the loss of both species. Rare exceptions might exist with professional aviculturists, or if a species dwindles down to only a precious few birds, but this is seldom the case with most hobbyist birdkeepers.

One option, if you are trying to avoid chance breedings between any of your birds is to house the males and the females separately. The birds can still socialize if you wish when you let them out for their daily exercise, should they be in smaller cages or pens, then separated again when play-time is over. Supervised playtime can always discourage a chance breeding.

Health Care

Though avian medicine has made many advances in treating the major diseases found in birds, the emphasis is still placed on prevention, especially when keeping multiple birds in a collection. Most major diseases are infectious and can be easily transmitted by conditions brought on by infrequent cleaning routines, feather dander, and dust particles from bird droppings and other airborne routes. Keep all cages and aviaries clean on a routine basis; wash up and disinfect your hands between servicing cages or aviaries and keep separate utensils and accessories for each aviary (keep an extra set to use when the current accessories are ready for cleaning). Talk to your avian veterinarian about vaccinations and any other precautions that might be helpful. It is always easier to prevent disease than to have to go through the time, expense, and heartache of treating a disease outbreak among your flock.

Preventing Disease

By nature, birds in the wild try to hide or mask symptoms; likewise, caged birds do not show signs of illness until they have become very ill. Once a caged bird begins to show symptoms it can be quite sick and in need of immediate medical attention. The sooner you get such a bird to the veterinarian, the better the chance for recovery. Some illnesses progress so far that a bird must be seen the same day, or it may not be able to survive a two- or three-day wait. It is a good idea to have a backup plan with an alternate veterinarian should your primary veterinarian be unable to

In parrots, good health can be determined by a number of factors: energy level, respiration, eyes, droppings, and feather condition.

accommodate you right away. Most avian veterinarians will try to fit in a patient, however, especially if they believe it is in need of immediate attention.

Owners should carefully observe and learn what their bird looks like when it is healthy. Observe a bird's posture while it is healthy and study how it sits on the perch. Is its back line and tail more or less "straight" or is it continuously pumping its tail alone, or in combination with a gaping beak showing labored breathing? Is its tail "hinged" downward at an angle, with its body feathers fluffed up? Does it continue to sneeze or make pumping motions with its neck in an effort to regurgitate? Study its face, are its eyes and nostrils clear? Look at the consistency of its droppings and get an idea of the number that is normal for your bird. Have the droppings changed dramatically in color or consistency? Except for those times when it is eating certain fruits and vegetables, a bird's droppings should remain relatively the same. However, if you have fed

Although some owners trim their birds' nails themselves, many prefer to have a veterinarian do the job.

Expert Advice

Keep double sets of dishes. When the first set is dirty, switch to clean items, then wash and store the first set for future use.

beet tops or red Swiss chard, do not be alarmed to see some red-purple stained droppings, which are the result of these vegetables passing through. No one knows the normal behavior and appearance of your birds better than you. Become an active observer so that you can let your veterinarian know exactly what changes have occurred, which will increase your bird's chances immensely.

Hygiene

The best method of preventing disease is good hygiene. Basic cleaning with soap and water cannot be emphasized strongly enough. *Always* wash your hands after visiting the bathroom. Birds are susceptible to human bacteria, which can be fatal to avian species. Not enough can be said about the virtues of handwashing before feeding, watering, and servicing cages. Conscientious breeders will disinfect their hands between aviaries or different rooms where they keep birds.

It is critically important to keep all food and water vessels clean. Use an appropriate disinfectant to clean your birds' cages, toys, feed bowls, perches, or any other items they come in contact with. Follow instructions on the bottle and rinse and dry thoroughly.

Cleanliness is the most important means of preventing disease. Cages should be cleaned daily and thoroughly cleaned at least weekly.

If a dish is dirty and you don't have a clean one on hand, old-fashioned soap and water goes a long way. Some birdkeepers use a gentle, dishwashing detergent to wash out dishes, then spray with a bird disinfectant, letting it soak for the allotted time, then rinse thoroughly before refilling. There is no reason for water cups to have foreign matter imbedded in the corners. To clean difficult jobs, use a scouring pad reserved for your birds, and remove all matter before disinfecting. Then toss the pad away. It is better to discard such items, because they can harbor germs and it will cost you a lot more in veterinary bills than the added cost of supplies if your birds become

---

Expert Advice

Prevent the spread of disease by using separate or new cleaning materials each time a cage is cleaned or a drinker is washed and refilled. Paper towels are excellent for soaping up with dishwashing detergent and cleaning water dishes; toss them out and use a fresh towel for the next water cup to be cleaned.

A pet carrier is one of the safest and most comfortable ways to transport a bird to the veterinarian.

sick. Many distributors sell disinfectant sprays that are appropriate for birds. If you can't find one, you can use bleach diluted in water (one-half cup of bleach to a gallon of water) to soak dirty dishes. Be certain to rinse and dry thoroughly before storing.

Bathing

Bathing birds on a regular basis, once a week in cooler weather and more frequently in warmer weather, can aid in their effort to keep a tight, clean, plumage. Good plumage and feather condition helps birds stay healthy by keeping out drafts and exposing their bodies to unfavorable temperatures. Whether you use a pressure pump to spray birds or a hand-held atomizer (the kind used for plants), reserve it for the birds only. Spray with only clean, cool or warm water, adding nothing to the water. If you can train your pet to accompany you into the shower, it can enjoy a real "rainforest shower"; to comfortably accommodate your bird, you may consider purchasing some of the shower perches made especially for parrots.

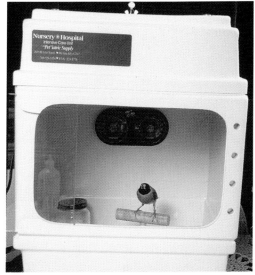

A sick bird should immediately be isolated from other birds. Be prepared with an incubation or hospital cage for such an unfortunate occasion.

Veterinary Visits

Should your bird become sick and require a visit to the veterinarian, there are some important precautions to take. For its own safety during the trip you may wish to place the bird in a pet carrier. Line the carrier with a soft towel, covered by paper towels, and include some millet spray and a piece of fruit, such as an orange, for moisture. Remove any water, as it will spill during transport and only serve to further chill the bird. Cover the carrier with one or more towels, depending upon the outside temperature. The bird will have plenty of air inside to breathe during transport, and the towels can shelter the bird from unfamiliar or upsetting bright lights, such as car headlights, should you have to travel at night. Most importantly, the towels will shelter the bird from drafts and help to keep it warm. As stated earlier, heat can be a life-saving measure for birds. If your bird has already been on heat, try wrapping the heating pad in the towel encasing the carrier, so that you can plug in the heating pad upon arrival. Using a hot water bottle might be a second alternative.

As always, preventing illness is much easier than curing a sick bird. However, the faster you get a sick bird in for treatment, the better the odds are for a full recovery.

Taming and Training

Keeping a trained, tame bird is a joy for both bird and owner, as it nourishes a growing bond of trust and love. Nearly any bird can be tamed, although some may take more time and patience on the part of the owner. However, that patience will be rewarded many times over by the sheer enjoyment of sharing one another's company. There is nothing sadder than an untrained bird sitting trapped inside a cage, unable to enjoy the freedom of interacting with its owner. Once trained, it is easier to proceed to teach a bird to talk, or learn tricks, and most important, to experience a lifetime of mutual love and affection.

Taming Techniques

For the first few sessions, it is best to keep the bird in a small room such as a bedroom or bathroom, with all mirrors covered and all windows and doors shut. If possible, obtain a young bird, just weaned, or a handfed baby that is already familiar with being handled. Although handfed birds are often sold as tame babies, they have yet to build a bond with their human owner, which requires time and patience. However, once your bird learns to trust you and it builds confidence in your relationship, a strong bond will begin to develop. If you are not able to secure a handfed baby, try to obtain a bird that has not long been separated from its parents but is fully weaned and able to eat on its own.

Older birds may be a challenge to train—some may come with their own emotional scars or issues and may require a great deal more time and patience from their new owners. Success with older birds comes most easily to those who have some experience in this area. This does not mean

Training is a great way to spend more time with your birds. Make the most of it and enjoy the process.

that an older bird cannot be tamed, but it may mean that a new owner's expectations may not be fully met; in that case, both bird and handler may end up unhappy. Some birds that were originally handfed may no longer be tame if they have been without human contact and ignored for long periods of time. Daily handling and gentleness by patient trainers will often restore these birds.

With a new bird it is best to choose one person in the family to be the trainer so the bird can become familiar with one person while becoming accustomed to its new surroundings. Keeping the bird in one small room, such as a bedroom, for at least the first few training sessions can be helpful in the beginning. Later on, once the bird is acclimated, it can be brought out to another room and slowly introduced to other family members and everyday activities.

When you bring your new bird home, set it up in a cage with all its feed and accessories and leave it alone for a short while to familiarize itself with its cage. Some birds are very curious right from the start, but others may be wary and require several days before eating normally and settling in to a new home.

Always move slowly and deliberately around a new bird. Speak in soft, comforting tones so it may familiarize itself with the sound of your voice. Don't make any sudden movements or loud noises that may frighten it.

Spend time each day training your new bird and speak gently to it in between sessions. If it is a small- to medium-size bird and it is not yet tame, start by slowly moving your hand toward the cage door, letting it rest there while talking gently. It is helpful to consistently associate your hand with a positive reinforcement such as a favorite food—a piece of apple, peanut, or sunflower seed, for example. Later on, once you build a bond between you and your bird, you may wish to change the food reinforcement to a social reward such as enthusiastic praise for an accomplished task.

Once the bird is at ease, you can begin to approach it with your hand. Extend your hand and move it slowly toward the bird, pressing gently under the bird's belly, inward and upward, forcing it slightly off-balance so that it will instinctively step up on to your hand. Talk

Expert Advice

Wing clipping should only be done by an experienced bird handler or avian veterinarian. If done improperly, a bird could be injured or develop ingrown or blood feathers, which can endanger its life if one is later dislodged and allowed to bleed. Wing clipping does not hurt a bird, it is like getting a haircut, and it can help prevent a bird from flying away and becoming permanently lost.

to the bird encouragingly and eventually move your hand around.

Repeat this procedure until you are able to bring the bird forward on your hand to the door and out of the cage. If, however, the bird is attempting to bite, it is best to keep your fingers rolled tight into a fist and present your hand with knuckles down, so that it cannot get a grip on you. This should be done in a non-threatening manner below the bird's chest.

Some birds only respond when they are outside their cage, which they regard as their personal territory, and may do better with training sessions on a playstand, provided their wings are clipped.

There are many different opinions on the best wing clip; however, it is generally agreed that all or most of the ten primary flight feath-

With some time, your bird should trust you enough to step onto your hand and be moved away from its cage or perch.

ers should be cut. Cutting the primaries on both wings may slow a bird down, but leaving the outer two or three primaries will look better and give a bird the appearance of looking flighted. The North American Parrot Society allows parrots to be exhibited at bird shows with clipped wings as a safety precaution, cutting the first seven flight feathers on each wing, and leaving the outer three

Consult with a breeder or veterinarian about the best style of wing clip for your bird.

flight feathers intact. Cutting the flight feathers on only one side can disorient a bird's flight course; however, some very strong flyers such as cockatiels require both wings to be clipped to really slow them down. Leaving the outer primary feathers intact enables a bird to break its fall if it lands on a hard surface such as a floor. Carpeting does provide better protection, but wing clips are still warranted for safety and to enhance hand-training sessions when a bird realizes it cannot fly away from its new owner.

When taming larger birds, it is best to start with a stick instead of your finger. Slowly move a stick or dowel toward the bird, speaking to the bird gently, until you are able to place the stick under its belly. Gently push the stick inward and upward, forcing the bird off-balance and making it step up on to the stick. It may take several minutes to accomplish this, take your time and be patient.

Once you have the bird stick trained, replace the stick with your finger. To accomplish this, just turn the stick backward while gripping the stick with your other free hand. This action will force the bird to move forward onto your "free" hand, which is grasping the center of the stick. Reward the bird with a food treat or kind word. Do not be afraid if your parrot first grips your fingers with its beak before moving forward. Your parrot is not intending to bite you; it is merely using its beak as its "third foot," which parrots routinely use whenever climbing from one point to another. It helps them steady themselves and gain their balance so they can continue gripping with their feet as they climb.

Parrots use their beak as a "third foot" and will test the perch—or hand—they are about to step onto. This is not biting.

Repeat this step until your bird is comfortable climbing onto your hand, then eventually begin to move around the room. Soon, your parrot will learn to ride on your shoulder, and in time can be taught to fly to you, as well as perform other commands you may wish to teach. Always remember, however, never to take a bird out of its cage without checking to see that all windows are closed, and remind everyone in the house not to open the front door until the bird is returned to its cage, unless the bird has a wing clip you can completely trust.

Food treats can be used as rewards during training, although you should be careful not to overfeed fattening foods.

Training Treats

Special food treats can be reserved for rewarding birds during taming or for training. Use such treats and specialty products sparingly, as too many can be fattening, which will lead to poor health. As with most things in life, moderation is the wisest way to proceed.

Keep in mind that some species, such as Amazons, Galahs, and budgerigars, are known to put on weight very easily. This does not mean that you must deny these birds, it only cautions owners to keep an eye on these species or any other bird that may tend to put on extra weight. Ideally, the best way to monitor your bird's weight, and therefore its health, is to purchase a gram scale and weigh your bird on a weekly basis. Your avian veterinarian can guide you on what is a reasonable weight for your bird.

Teaching to Talk

Some species have a reputation for their talking ability, most notably the familiar greater Indian Hill Mynah bird, the African Grey parrot, the Mexican Double Yellow-headed Amazon parrot, and the Yellow-naped Amazon parrot. Though these species may have remarkable abilities to mimic and build a vocabulary, it is often the individual bird, rather than an entire species, that may excel at this ability. For example, one might find a particular Blue-fronted Amazon parrot to be a superior talker to a certain Double Yellow-headed Amazon. In general, most Double Yellow-headed Amazons will be superior mimics to Blue-fronteds. As a rule, the larger the bird, the stronger and clearer the voice; again there may be exceptions among some individuals.

A tame bird is generally easier to train to talk than one that has not been tamed. Be patient, results take time and repetition.

It is a lot easier to teach your bird to talk once it has become hand-tame and trusting. Try to keep the training sessions on a regular schedule and at the same time each day. To begin, select one word with no more than two syllables, such as "hello," and repeat it slowly and distinctly in a clear voice over and over. Birds are more likely to mimic higher, feminine voices. While training, you may wish to remove any distracting toys or mirrors, or place the bird where environmental distractions will not interfere.

Some birds are allowed freedom in a home. However, be aware of dangers to your bird—and to your furniture and other possessions.

Repetition is key to training a successful talker, but it is good to remember that birds generally have a limited attention span of only a few minutes. Therefore, to facilitate the process, you might want to purchase any of the creative training tapes on the market, or create your own and play it each morning before going to work for about 10 to 15 minutes. When you get home you can play the tape again for your bird's second lesson. Finally, when you are energized after dinner, you can give your bird its third lesson in person.

It may take several weeks or months before your bird says its first word. Do not be discouraged and do not give up. Once it learns to

It's fine for your bird to consider you as part of its flock, but you should always be the dominant member.

say its first word, the rest is easy and future lessons will come pouring out. Following the first word, you might wish to teach the bird its name (for example, "Hello, Peter!") then go on to other phrases with three or four syllables, and so on. A bird's success will be determined by the effort made on your behalf. Therefore, the talent lies not only in the bird, but also in its teacher.

Your Relationship to the Flock

As with any social group of animals, a dominance hierarchy is key to survival. Parrots in the wild travel, find food, and nest together in pairs or flocks, because there is safety in numbers. Yet, they also work out such important matters as defining and protecting their territory and deciding who gets to eat first and in what order. Tame parrots consider their owners as a part of their flock, and it is natural for them to want to establish a flock hierarchy to include their owner and perhaps other humans in the household.

The dominant or top-ranking individual is referred to as the alpha or flock leader. If training has proceeded correctly, the trainer will be perceived as the flock leader by the birds. However, many times training is either mishandled or this concept is poorly understood, and human owners tend to give this higher status away to their pet bird, which continues to command the household.

As outlined earlier, the correct method to train a bird is by using positive reinforcement such as a food reward. Later, once the bird learns what is expected of it, food rewards can be substituted by praise, which will only work if a successful bond is created between the bird and owner. If a bird demonstrates a negative behavior, it is best to ignore the behavior, but offer a reward for the next immediate positive action the bird demonstrates. For example, should a bird attempt to bite your finger, as painful as it may be, resist the temptation to react negatively. Instead, twist your wrist to force the bird off your hand, and should it land on its playstand and interact with anything on it, say "good boy!" By reinforcing a different behavior, you avoid making a negative incident of the unwelcome biting behavior. Research has shown that any reinforcement, whether positive or negative, tends to encourage a bird to repeat that act again in the future. If a behavior is ignored, it is less likely to be repeated. Of course, this process takes patience, but it is well worth the effort.

Expert Advice

At no time should negative punishment, such as striking a bird anywhere on its head or body, ever be used. Negative punishment never works; it only contributes to distrust, and a bird will never forget an incident in which it was punished.

Some birds are allowed freedom in a home. However, be aware of dangers to your bird—and to your furniture and other possessions.

A common behavior that can occur once parrots pair up, whether you intentionally plan to breed or not, is the event of transferred aggression. Bonded parrots usually demonstrate transferred aggression, where one of the pair (usually the male) may attack its mate or chicks if threatened by an outside stimulus. This outside stimulus may be you or something unfamiliar that stimulates the bird to dislodge his aggression at the nearest target. Unfortunately, this can sometimes be its mate. Other times, it may even be you, its keeper, with whom under ordinary circumstances the bird would be most gentle. Do not take it personally. This is natural and is only hormones at work as nature has intended. Remember, parrots in the wild often have to defend their territory against intruders and they would not normally have an owner bringing them food or visiting them. Once the breeding season is over and hormone levels return to their natural levels, your parrots will usually return to their tame, lovable dispositions.

Special Needs Birds

S ometimes bird hobbyists run into unusual or special circumstances that they have not encountered before. It is best to consult others with knowledge in this area who may be able to provide some insightful advice. Some excellent resources, in addition to your avian veterinarian, are local and national bird clubs; animal shelters or veterinary hospitals who can refer you to bird behaviorists or local breeders on their recommended list; or specialty books and magazines that may carry further information on such topics.

Geriatrics

Some species, especially the larger parrots such as African Greys, cockatoos, macaws, and Amazon parrots, can live many years, some outliving their owners. Though it can be difficult to determine the precise age of many birds, unless they are wearing a seamless, closed, traceable leg band that can be verified with a birth date, it may be hard to know just how old a bird is. Some species show advanced age by their coloring. For example, some of the Amazon parrots such as Double Yellow-headed show advancing age as the entire head turns yellow; the Red-lored Amazon also shows its age when the red over its lores extends down through its yellow cheeks causing an orange coloration. Some birds show some scaliness on their feet.

Like people, birds can become ill during their lifetime and should be seen by a veterinarian. If a bird develops arthritis, owners might try and be more patient about commanding their bird to step up on their hand or perform tricks they have learned. Some owners regularly spray mist their birds periodically, or take them with them into the shower. Older birds that previously enjoyed their bathtime but that try to escape this effort might be feeling the effects of arthritis or other maladies and should not be forced.

Many parrots can outlive their owners, so bird owners might want to provide for their birds by including them in their will. Special provisions should be made, or beloved and valued birds may not end up where the owner intended.

Handicapped Birds

Bird owners are occasionally tempted to take in a handicapped bird that no one wants, or they may through the course of breeding produce a bird that is not fully functional. The latter is rare, and most handicapped bird stories usually involve some sort of accident or illness.

Making the decision to keep a handicapped bird should be given great thought and consideration. Caring for a handicapped bird is a serious commitment that will last for the life of that bird. Depending upon the age and species, that could amount to a great number of years

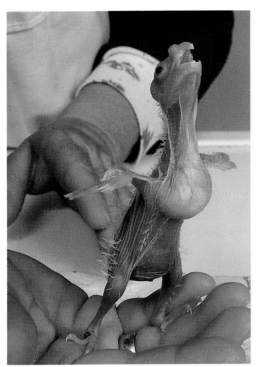

Beginners should not take in a handicapped bird or one with special needs. Such a bird requires specialized care and attention.

and require a lot of work on the part of the caregiver. However, the bond between such a bird and its owner can be very deep.

If you are unable to make the commitment to provide the necessary care for a bird in need of extra assistance, then it may be wise to consider talking to your veterinarian for other placement with someone who is willing to provide the care necessary, or to consider euthanasia. There are many cases of handicapped birds living happy lives with their owners and other birds. Each case, however, must be considered separately, as the circumstances are unique to each.

Rescued Birds

Helping to rescue unwanted birds is to be applauded, but be cautious not to bring birds into your collection that have not been through quarantine. As stated in earlier sections, all birds must go through quarantine; without it you are putting your birds at risk. If you must take in a bird, keep it at a neighbor's house or on a separate air system until the quarantine period is over. If you intend to keep the rescued bird, it should also be given an initial exam by your avian veterinarian.

Many bird clubs across the country keep special adoption programs running year-round, placing such birds with club members who pay a fee to cover its veterinary visit, or awarding them to homes thought to be best for the bird. Many animal hospitals can put you in touch with a local bird club, where members can explain how they run their programs and whether or not they provide temporary foster homes for rescued birds.

Handfeeding and First Aid

Occasionally, bird owners are faced with handfeeding in an emergency, which usually involves either an injured or sick adult or a newborn chick that is not being fed by its parents. Both are emergency situations; if you are inexperienced in handfeeding, you are better off seeking the advice of someone who is knowledgeable in this area.

If you are dealing with a sick or injured bird, the first step is to provide a heated environment. Birds are unable to digest food unless their body temperature is comfortable, and heating the environment is always the first step in administering any first aid. Use a hospital cage or create one by placing a covered heating pad under a cage with the tray removed. Newspaper can be placed on top of the heating pad before the cage is set back down. Wrap several towels around the top, back, sides, and lower front of the cage, leaving the upper front

Rescued birds can make wonderful pets; many can be found through adoption programs or at bird sanctuaries.

portion open. This will create a very warm environment for the bird. However, carefully monitor the bird to be certain it does not overheat. Birds that are too hot will flatten down their feathers, hold their wings out in an effort to cool off, and start to pant with a gaping beak. Birds that are too cold or chilled will exhibit loose feathering and be puffed out in an effort to stay warm.

One of the reasons to first apply heat in any attempt to supply first aid, is that a bird will spend

Expert Advice

I once owned a domestically raised Rose-breasted cockatoo (known as a Galah in its native Australia) that for the last 11 years of its life was paraplegic. "Sundoll" rested comfortably on a platform built especially for her, with side bars, positioned where a normal perch would be placed so she felt safe and comfortable. The platform was covered with layers of towels, changed several times a day to keep her clean. She was very social and greatly enjoyed her daily grooming session and special treats during her daily time on the sofa for a change of scenery. In good weather, we sat outside to enjoy the sun and wind on her face, as she was unable to fly. Sundoll finally succumbed to an extremely rare parathyroid tumor, which had crippled her, yet I believe her additional 11 years with me were so much more intense and loving than the earlier nine years spent in the aviary with the other birds. However, the heartache of losing her was even more traumatic because of the extremely close bond.

Handfeeding is a task best left to those with experience. Consult with a breeder or veterinarian before attempting to feed a baby bird.

all of its energy trying to stay warm and have little energy left to fight off disease. By providing heat, you help the bird conserve its energy so that it can start to fight off illness. If you can put a thermometer in the upper part of the cage out of reach of the bird, you will know the precise temperature. Ideally, birds respond best in 85 to 90° F.

If a bird has broken its leg or wing, remove all the perches from the cage and place food and water vessels nearby. Be careful not to place the water dish on top of the heating pad, and use a hook-on cup to avoid spills. Birds that are weak and have difficulty sitting up might need to lean on a small, rolled up soft face cloth.

Try placing the bird's favorite soft foods within easy reach, including millet spray, cooked corn niblets, whole wheat bread, and other easy-to-eat items it may know and like. You may even offer the bird a mixture of a handfeeding diet, holding it up in a separate cup to see if it will eat it. Otherwise, you can attempt to offer the formula through a syringe (providing the bird was hand-raised and is not frightened by a syringe) or by spoon. Never force a bird to eat and never force formula from a syringe into a bird's beak or it could choke and aspirate the material.

If the bird is not interested in eating it should be seen by an avian veterinarian right away, as chances are it will require medication. Your veterinarian will probably take a culture or gram stain, administer an appropriate medication, and call you with the results of the test. If it is indicated, the veterinarian might decide to switch to something more effective. However, if you decide to self-medicate the bird, you waste valuable time and could lose the bird if the medication and amount you choose is ineffective.

In the event that you discover a chick that is not being fed by its parents, you may elect to hand-feed it. Some bird breeders believe that chicks rejected by their parents are weak or sick, and the adults are responding to nature's "survival of the fittest" tactics where the weak or sick are not cared for. Yet, many aviculturists have stories of sick birds that go on to have strong, healthy lives and offspring.

The decision to hand-feed is also dependent upon the amount of time and the commitment you are willing to make. Most baby birds less than 10 days of age must be fed every two hours, with a four to six hour stretch at night. As chicks age, they can eventually go eight hours overnight and be fed again first thing in the morning at 6:00 or 7:00 a.m. Although the schedule continues to improve and the number of feeds eventually lessen, some birds may take longer to finish feeding than others, depending upon the species, until they are fully weaned and are eating on their own. For example, where the average cockatiel may take two months, a Hyacinth macaw may take as long as four months to wean. It often helps if the feeder has someone else to assist with one or more shifts so they are not deprived of sleep or tire from the strain of keeping up with feedings.

There are a number of excellent brands of handfeeding formula on the market today, scientifically formulated and tested on large numbers of birds. Follow manufacturer's directions precisely and do not add any other items that will change the balance of the formulas and prove detrimental to the chicks. The instructions will reveal how to prepare and heat the formula as well as give advice on amounts, number of feedings, and other helpful information. Never save leftover formula, always discard it and start with fresh.

It is best to take out a limited amount of dry formula and store it in a sealed container out of the heat and light for daily use. Seal the bag tightly and store the rest away in the freezer, which will extend the life of the product. In the event of an emergency, if you have no handfeeding formula on hand and pet stores are closed, purchase some baby cereal from the market, (for example, a multi-grain cereal and a jar of baby cereal with oatmeal, apple, and banana added), mix and cook over the stove, making certain to add enough water to produce a thin, soup-like mixture. Very tiny chicks can only take a thinner gruel. If you are inexperienced, seek the advice of someone experienced, as handfeeding is difficult at best. Keep the chicks warm, and feed only when the crop empties to avoid the possibility of impacted crop. Ideally, it is best to obtain an avian handfeeding formula and seek professional or veterinary advice.

Unweaned Birds

Though the idea of getting and handfeeding a baby parrot or other species might sound tempting, it is not always in the best interest of the bird or the buyer to do so. Unless you have experience handfeeding, you can end up losing a bird. Even breeders who routinely hand-feed smaller birds have lost a larger bird due to inexperience, and perhaps overconfidence by assuming the challenge would be the same.

Breeders who sell unweaned birds are usually looking to unload their birds quickly, discard the responsibility of weaning, and collect their money without risking the possibility of losing a bird before it gains its independence. Many times, new owners are not even given proper instruction on how to feed chicks: how much to feed, how often to feed, or guidelines and markers of progress. The only time a breeder should release an unweaned bird is under special circumstances, such as going to another breeder or owner who has been successful with feeding the very same species in the past.

Breeders who are concerned about the birds they produce and place in new homes will only sell weaned birds. Weaned birds are birds that consistently eat adult foods and are able to fill their crops on their own every night. The age of weaning varies by the species of the bird. Even within the same species there can be some individual variation. However, these variations should not be extreme.

If a chick continues to cry and beg for food, and refuses to eat on its own, chances are you have an unweaned baby that you will have to finish handfeeding. First, try and coax the bird to eat on its own. Though shyer species such as cockatiels and some others take some time to settle down in new homes, handfed babies

Although most birds are capable of traveling, friends or qualified pet-sitters can care for birds in your absence.

A gram scale used on a daily basis will help monitor your baby bird's weight gain and health.

usually adjust more easily. If you suspect your new bird is not weaned, and it continues to beg for food, contact the seller for advice on its age and what to feed it, or seek out the advice of a handfeeding specialist.

Pet-sitters

Whether or not your birds have special needs, you may find it necessary to leave your birds in the care of someone else when you need to go away. Today, there are a number of bonded pet-sitters who make their living looking after and caring for other people's pets. Pet-sitters can be found through many sources, such as magazines that cater to bird owners, bird club newsletters, local advertising, your avian veterinarian, and even friends and relatives.

It is usually best to get a pet-sitter from someone you know who recommends the individual as a reliable sitter. Just as with baby-sit-

ters, you may require references before engaging their services. It may be wise to set up an appoint-
ment to meet with the sitter and introduce the sitter to the birds they will be caring for. This meeting will be helpful in a number of ways: it will familiarize your birds with the new caretaker; it will
introduce the pet-sitter to your birds, and it will provide you with the opportunity to question the
sitter to see how familiar they are with birds and their care.

Do not be shy about asking the sitter questions, or asking about their experience caring for birds.
Think of it like an interview. If you are uncomfortable with the pet-sitter, you do not have to make
a future engagement and can look for someone else.

Once you select your pet-sitter and have negotiated the charges and know what to expect, do not
hesitate to go over the needs of all of your birds and what you expect from the sitter while you are
away. Some sitters have limits, but others are happy to do additional chores such as water your
plants or take in the newspaper while you are away. It is always best to put your instructions in
writing for your sitter to refer to. The instructions should be specific, and should specify the needs
for each cage, flight, or aviary in their care. By putting everything in writing, you guarantee you
have not overlooked any items. Include your avian veterinarian's phone number and the number
of another bird person, in case of an emergency. The instructions can be saved, updated, and used
again in the future.

Resources

AFA Watchbird

American Federation of Aviculture, Inc.
P.O. Box 56218
Phoenix, AZ 85079
www.afa.birds.org
The AFA is a nonprofit organization dedicated to the promotion of aviculture and the conservation of avian wildlife through the encouragement of captive breeding programs, scientific research, and the education of the general public. The AFA publishes a bi-monthly magazine called *AFA Watchbird*.

Association of Avian Veterinarians

P.O. Box 811720
Boca Raton, FL 33481
561-393-8901561-393-8902
www.aav.org
AAV membership is comprised of veterinarians from private practice, zoos, universities and industry, veterinary educators, researchers and technicians, and veterinary students. Serves as resource for bird owners who are looking for certified avian veterinarians.

Avicultural Society of Australia, Inc.

80 Harris Road
Elliminyt
Victoria 3249
Australia
The Avicultural Society of Australia is one of the oldest avicultural societies in Australia and welcomes membership applications from persons interested in birds, their welfare and care, both in captivity and in the wild.

Bird Talk

Subscription Dept.
P.O. Box 57347
Boulder, CO 80323
www.animalnetwork.com
Bird Talk is a monthly magazine noted for its directory of avian breeders, as well as its informative articles and columns on health care, conservation, and behavior.

Bird Times

Pet Publishing, Inc.
7-L Dundas Circle
Greensboro, NC 27407
www.birdtimes.com
Bird Times magazine is a source of entertaining and authoritative information about birds. Articles include bird breed profiles, medical reports, training advice, bird puzzles, and stories about special birds.

The Gabriel Foundation

P.O. Box 11477
Aspen, CO 81612
www.thegabrielfoundation.org
A nonprofit organization promoting education, rescue, adoption, and sanctuary for parrots.

The NAPS Journal

North American Parrot Society, Inc.
P.O. Box 404
Salem, OH 44460
www.drzoolittle.com
Formed in 1995, NAPS sponsors bird shows and aims to put fun back into showing for exhibitors. NAPS members are individual pet owners, breeders with small and large aviaries, show judges, veterinarians, and people who enjoy exhibiting. Members can purchase closed bands from NAPS.

The Parrot Society, Inc.

108b Fenlake Road
Bedford, MK42 OEU
England
The Parrot Society promotes the keeping, breeding, care, study, and conservation of parrots.

Index

Index

Photo Credits

Joan Balzarini: 10T, 29T, 39, 50T, 52, 60

Isabelle Francais: 4, 14, 12T, 16B, 17, 18, 19, 20, 22, 23, 24, 25, 26, 27, 28T, 29B, 30, 32, 33, 35T, 36, 37, 42B, 43, 46, 48, 49, 50B, 51B, 53, 54, 56, 57, 58, 60T

Michael Gilroy:8T, 9B, 11T, 51T

Robert Pearcy: 12B

John Tyson:6, 8B, 9T, 10B, 11B, 13, 16T, 28B, 30, 34, 35B, 38, 40, 42T, 44

CONTENTS

by SAADIA FARUQI   illustrated by DEBBY RAHMALIA

For Adam —SF
For Alesha —DR

Raintree is an imprint of Capstone Global Library Limited, a company incorporated in England and Wales having its registered office at 264 Banbury Road, Oxford, OX2 7DY – Registered company number: 6695582

www.raintree.co.uk
myorders@raintree.co.uk

Text © Capstone Global Library Limited 2024
The moral rights of the proprietor have been asserted.

Designed by Kay Fraser and Tracy Davies
Original illustrations © Capstone Global Library Limited 2024
Originated by Capstone Global Library Ltd

978 1 3982 5296 7

British Library Cataloguing in Publication Data
A full catalogue record for this book is available from the British Library.

Printed and bound in India.

LET'S LEARN SOME URDU!

Ali and his family speak both English and Urdu, a language from Pakistan. Now you'll know some Urdu too!

ABBA (also baba) father

AMMA (also mama) mother

BHAI brother

DADA grandfather on father's side

DADI grandmother on father's side

SALAAM hello

SHUKRIYA thank you

☆ ChapteR 1 ☆

BORED

It was raining outside. Ali's class was stuck in the gym for playtime.

"I'm so bored!" Ali groaned.

"Yeah," Zack agreed. "There's nothing to do inside!"

Yasmin saw some boxes and peeked inside. "Ooh, art supplies!" she said. She took out some paper and crayons and started colouring.

Ali thought colouring was boring. He watched Yasmin work. Was there something fun he could do with that paper?

"I know!" Ali suddenly

shouted. "Let's make paper

aeroplanes!"

Yasmin looked up and

frowned. "I don't know how to."

Ali grinned. "Don't worry," he said. "I'll help you. I'm an expert!"

He took a piece of paper and folded it carefully. Once, twice, three times. He made sure the creases were very sharp.

Ta-da! Ali held up his paper aeroplane.

"Cool!" Zack said. "Can you please make me one too?"

"Me too!" said Emma.

☆ Chapter 2 ☆
THE CONTEST

Ali took more papers from the box and folded more aeroplanes.

He didn't rush. He had to be careful and neat. If he made a mistake, the aeroplane wouldn't fly as far.

Soon, there was a pile of aeroplanes for his friends to choose from.

Yasmin grabbed her crayons.
"I'm going to draw a design on
mine!" she said.

"Great idea!" Ali replied. Art
wasn't boring when there were
planes involved!

Ali added white racing stripes

to his. Yasmin drew flowers on

hers. Emma's had polka dots.

Zack's had a fire-breathing

dragon!

Then Ali showed his friends
how to fly their planes.

"You have to hold up
your plane like this and lean
forward," he said. "And you
have to throw hard."

"Let's have a contest!" Zack
suggested. "Whoever's plane flies
the furthest wins!"

"Okay!" Ali said. He was the
expert, and he was ready!

Emma went first. Her plane

flew towards the basketball hoop.

"Yay!" she said.

Then it was Zack's turn. His

plane went even further. "Beat

that!" Zack said.

Yasmin was third. She smiled
nervously.

"You can do it, Yasmin!" Ali
cheered.

Yasmin aimed carefully, then threw. Her plane landed all the way in the stands!

"Wow!" everyone cried.

ChapteR 3

AND THE WINNER IS . . .

Finally, it was Ali's turn. He wasn't worried. He built the best aeroplanes. He would definitely win!

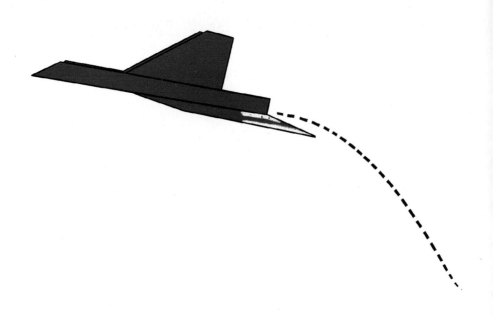

Ali threw his paper aeroplane

with all his might. It soared high

up. Then it dipped down. Then it

looped and twisted!

Everyone watched the plane. It

looped once more. Then it landed

. . . right behind Ali.

"Oh no!" Ali cried. This was terrible. He wasn't the winner. He'd come in last!

"I lost?" he said, surprised.

"No, you didn't, Ali," Yasmin said. "You're the winner, with me!"

"I am?" Ali asked.

Emma nodded. "She's right! You made our aeroplanes for us," she said.

"And you taught us the best way to fly," Zack added.

Ali started to feel better. He *did* know the most about building paper aeroplanes.

Yasmin clapped. "We both

win!" she cheered loudly.

"Teamwork!" Zack said, even

louder.

Ali pointed to the box of supplies. "Ready for another round?" he asked.

"Bring it on, co-pilot!" Yasmin replied.

JUST JOKING AROUND

How do rabbits travel?
By hare-plane

Why did the plane get sent to its room?
Because it had a bad altitude

Why did the teenager study on an aeroplane?
Because he wanted a higher education

What happens if you wear a watch on an aeroplane?
Time flies!

BUILD A PAPER AEROPLANE

Take a sheet of paper and follow the directions to make a paper aeroplane.

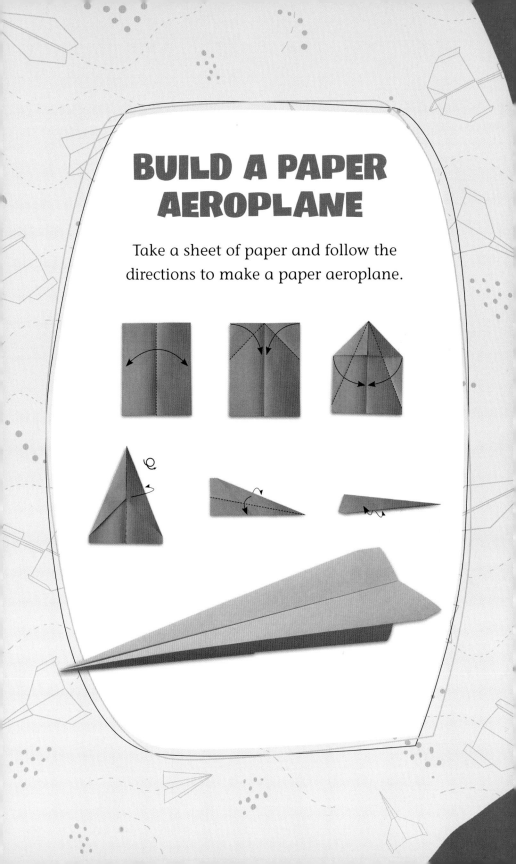

THINK BIG WITH ALI THE GREAT!

☆ Ali is frustrated that he doesn't win the paper aeroplane contest, even though he built all the planes. Can you relate to how Ali feels? How do you help yourself feel better when something seems unfair?

☆ Co-pilots are people who share the work and responsibility of flying a plane. The word "co-pilot" can also mean partner in a project or adventure. Think of a project or activity you would like to try. Who would you choose as your co-pilot, and why?

☆ About the authoR ☆

Saadia Faruqi is a Pakistani American writer, interfaith activist and cultural sensitivity trainer featured in *O, The Oprah Magazine*. Author of the Yasmin chapter book series, Saadia also writes other books for children, including *Yusuf Azeem Is Not a Hero*. Saadia is editor-in-chief of *Blue Minaret*, an online magazine of poetry, short stories and art. Besides writing, she also loves reading, binge-watching her favourite series and taking naps.

☆ About the iLLusTRatoR ☆

Debby Rahmalia is an illustrator based in Indonesia with a passion for storytelling. She enjoys creating diverse works that showcase an array of cultures and people. Debby's long-term dream was to become an illustrator. She was encouraged to pursue her dream after she had her first baby and has been illustrating ever since. When she's not drawing, she spends her time reading the books she illustrated to her daughter or wandering around the neighbourhood with her.

JOIN

ALI
THE
GREAT

on his adventures!

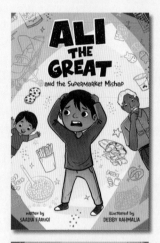

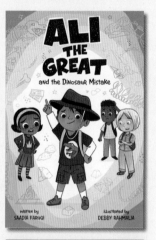

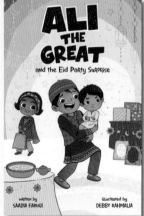